TRUE
FRIENDSHIP

True Friendship © 10Publishing 2013 Vaughan Roberts

Published by 10Publishing, a division of 10ofthose.com

Unit C, Tomlinson Road, Leyland, PR25 2DY

Email: info@10ofthose.com Website: www.10ofthose.com

ISBN: 978-1-909611-32-0

Unless otherwise indicated, all Scripture quotations are taken from the Holy Bible: New International Version.

Copyright © 1973, 1978, 1984 by International Bible Society.

Reprinted 2014, 2016 and 2017

Designed by Diane Bainbridge

Printed in Denmark by Nørhaven

TRUE FRIENDSHIP
WALKING SHOULDER TO SHOULDER

VAUGHAN ROBERTS

10 Publishing
a division of 10 of those.com

In grateful memory of Piers Cheyne (1965–2006)

Faithful friend for thirty-five years

CONTENTS

ACKNOWLEDGEMENTS

I am hugely thankful for all those who have shown me what true friendship looks like in practice. In particular I am grateful to Jonathan Carswell, Clare Heath-Whyte, Phil and Katy Jack, Matt Lloyd, Philip Moore, Ed Shaw and Pete Wilkinson for commenting on the first draft of this book, and to Josh Bell for his typing.

INTRODUCTION

'I'LL BE THERE FOR YOU'

Friends, the sitcom featuring six single people in their 20s living in New York, attracted huge audiences when it was first aired from the mid 1990s, and is still shown almost continuously on satellite channels throughout the world. What explains this phenomenal success? Perhaps the answer is found in the title of its theme song: 'I'll Be There For You'. Those words capture the dreams of a generation. David Schwimmer, one of the actors, has commented: 'It's a fantasy for a lot of people – having a group of friends who become like family.'[1]

For many that is all it is: a fantasy. Twenty per cent of adults admit to feeling lonely at any time and the same percentage say they have no friend with whom to discuss a personal problem.[2] Commenting on this widespread sense of isolation, Mother Teresa, who spent her life working with destitute people in Calcutta, said that the worst disease was not leprosy, AIDS or cancer, but loneliness.

It may be that as you begin this book you are painfully conscious of a lack of close friends. That has been my experience at times in the past, but my life has been immeasurably enriched and strengthened by deepening friendships in recent years. I should say right at the start that I claim no great wisdom on this subject and still consider myself a novice. I am hugely grateful for all I have learnt from the many friends who have loved me patiently and lived life alongside me. Even those who are most naturally gifted at friendship would say that they are still learning as together we sit under God's teaching in the Bible. My aim in this book is, therefore, certainly not to pass on my own thoughts on the subject, but to present wisdom from the Bible. All of us, whether we feel lonely or enjoy many close relationships, need to hear its challenge to live intimately connected lives, and how to give to and receive from others in that context.

A PLEA FOR PRAYERFUL READING

I am passionate about the subject of this book, both because of my own personal experience and, above all, because of the importance it is given in the Bible. I have deliberately kept the material as brief as possible to make it accessible, so it might be possible for you to read it in little more than an hour. Having said that, I hope you will give more time to it than that. You will gain most from the book if you pause to think and pray as you read. The questions at the end of each chapter are designed to help you do this, whether individually or with others.

It will soon become clear that I am writing with followers of Jesus Christ especially in mind, but I hope that some who would not call themselves Christians will also read this book. If that is you, I trust you will find some insights that will help you in your friendships, but my greatest longing is that you will come to enjoy what Christians believe is by far the greatest friendship of all: a relationship with God through Jesus Christ.

Vaughan Roberts

TRUE FRIENDSHIP IS CRUCIAL

1

THE HEART OF THE BIBLE'S MESSAGE

The theme of friendship takes us right to the heart of the Bible's message. God is relational. He has from eternity existed in a relationship of loving friendship within the Godhead: Father, Son and Holy Spirit. He created us in his image as relational beings, uniquely able to relate to him in love. Genesis 2 provides us with a picture of life as it was designed to be, with Adam and Eve enjoying perfect relationships with God, one another and the world around them, before everything was spoilt by their rejection of God's authority. A sense of aching nostalgia for what has been lost is evoked by the description of God walking in the cool of the garden in Genesis 3, with the implication that it has been his custom to take a daily stroll with his image-friend.

The easy intimacy between God and humanity is lost because of sin but, in his amazing grace, he still seeks relationship, calling out, 'Where are you?' (Genesis 3:9). This searching, divine love lies behind God's gospel plan to restore people to relationship with himself, which was promised and prefigured in the Old Testament and then fulfilled through Christ.

Throughout the Bible, God often calls those who belong to him his friends. The Lord spoke to Moses 'as a man speaks with his friend' (Exodus 33:11) and describes Abraham as 'my friend' (Isaiah 41:8). In criticizing Jesus as a 'friend of ... "sinners"' (Matthew 11:19), his enemies had seen the truth without recognizing the wonder of it. The disciples were deeply flawed men, and yet Jesus called them his 'friends' (Luke 12:4). We too can be friends of God, not because of any innate worthiness in us, but because of Christ's death for us on the cross. God's own son faced separation from his Father so that we, who do not deserve it, could be restored to friendship with him.

God's plan of salvation is designed not only to restore our vertical relationship with God, but also to create horizontal relationships of loving friendship between human beings in his family. He calls us to himself, not as individuals, but as members of a new community. Deep relationships can, and should, develop as we grow together in the church into the likeness of Christ, and serve together in mission. After Christ's return, there will be no marriage (Matthew 22:30), but great intimacy will be enjoyed in the beyond-sexuality delight of friendship with one another as God's people in the new creation.

READING THE BIBLE AS GOSPEL

This brief survey of the core of the Bible's teaching shows that friendship is not an optional extra, but is essential to our God-given humanity. Living unfriendly and friendless lives is both a rejection of God's purpose for us as his image, and a dehumanizing tragedy. Just as God is love, so he commands us to prioritize love in our lives by loving him and our neighbours (see Mark 12:30,31). This is not something we can do by ourselves, which explains the mess we so often make of our relationships. But, wonderfully, God is determined to change us by his Spirit so that we are transformed from being turned in on ourselves to reaching out in love to him and others. The Bible is not a self-help book with instructions for how we can improve our lives; rather, it is a proclamation of the gospel, the 'good news', which speaks of what God has done, is doing and will do by the Holy

17

Spirit for those who trust in Christ. It is important that we do not forget this gospel framework as we consider some of the Bible's detailed instructions about friendship. Reading the Bible as gospel gives us the proper motivation for friendship, real power to relate well to others and practical wisdom for how to do so.

'DOING LIFE WELL'

Some people are very good at navigating through life; they just seem to understand how the world works, and live accordingly. But others are forever getting into trouble; if there is a pit anywhere near, they will find it and fall into it. The difference between them is not usually a matter of intelligence: it is possible to have a massive intellect and still be inept at the basic business of living. Nor is it always a question of morality: two people can share exactly the same moral principles and seek to live by them, and yet one still manages to make a mess of their relationships, work and finances, while the other thrives in them. The difference, more often than not, concerns wisdom.

In the next few chapters, we will often look to the teaching of the book of Proverbs in the Old Testament as we consider God's teaching on friendship. Proverbs is a wisdom book, designed to teach us how to 'do life well'. Its foundation principle is stated in the introduction: 'The fear of the LORD is the beginning of knowledge' (Proverbs 1:7). The fundamental relationship in our life must be with the one true God, the sovereign Creator. The Bible insists that true wisdom begins when we 'fear' him: recognizing who he is and what he has done for us in Christ, and then responding with a worshipful, trusting submission. No friendship is more important than this relationship with God, which we will consider more at the end of the book.

While teaching the foundational importance of relating rightly to God, the book of Proverbs also stresses the vital significance of other relationships if we are to live wisely. In his book *Friendship*, which is the best I have read on the subject, Hugh Black writes: 'the book of Proverbs might almost be called a treatise on friendship – there is no book, even in classical literature, which so exalts the idea of friendship and is so anxious to have it truly valued and carefully kept'.[1] That is because the task of seeking wisdom, which is often so elusive, is a communal project which should not be undertaken on our own. Life is presented in Proverbs as a journey in which we are constantly faced with a choice between two paths: wisdom and folly. We need good friends who will travel with us, help us discern the right road to take and spur us on to keep walking down it. Such companions will immeasurably strengthen us: 'As iron sharpens iron, so one man sharpens another' (Proverbs 27:17).

'FELLOW TRAVELLERS'

In his essay on friendship, C.S. Lewis points out that while lovers are often seen face to face, delighting in one another, the characteristic pose of friends is side by side or shoulder to shoulder. Friendship begins, he suggests, when people discover a common interest or passion. It is found when we discover those travelling the same road as us, and decide to walk together.

Friendship is, in other words, based on shared goals. Aelred, a British monk in the twelfth century, who wrote a classic book on friendship,[2] distinguishes between three types, each of which is forged around a different kind of goal. 'Carnal friendship' is based on the shared pursuit of pleasure, whether it be a common delight in clubbing or golf. 'Worldly friendship' is based on mutual advantage, as when business partners work closely together. There need be nothing wrong with either type of relationship, depending on the goal and manner in which it is pursued, but Aelred believed that a third type of friendship was the deepest. This is 'spiritual friendship', which is grounded in a mutual commitment to follow Jesus Christ.

Over the years I have formed close bonds with fellow stamp collectors at school, as we shared the excitement of a new addition to our collections; with colleagues, as we have spurred each other on through the trials of exams; and with teammates, even in an individual sport such as squash, as we trained hard together and cheered for one another in matches. But my deepest friendships have been with other disciples of Christ.

Christians have the ultimate common passion and shared goal, which encompasses the whole of life. We have been called, as brothers and sisters, to belong to Christ's family, as we travel along the way of the cross throughout our lives, with our eyes fixed on the destination of the new creation to come, which Christ will introduce when he returns. It is a long journey, with many challenges along the road. We will often fall and need someone to pick us up; waver, and need another to spur us on. Let us resolve therefore to obey the Bible's instruction:

'let us consider how we may spur one another on towards love and good deeds ... let us encourage one another – and all the more as you see the Day approaching' (Hebrews 10:24,25).

Are you looking for opportunities to spur on others in this way? Too many Christians, even those who see one another regularly, relate with very little, if any, reference to their shared faith. Perhaps we need to take the initiative with some friends to ensure that the basis of our relationship is not simply 'carnal' or 'worldly', but above all, 'spiritual'. If you do not know how to start, why not suggest that you pray together, or ask questions which will open up spiritual conversation, such as:

'How is your Christian life going at the moment?'

'What are you finding especially encouraging?'

'What are some of the greatest challenges?'

We should take every opportunity to encourage any of our fellow travellers in the Christian journey, but there will need to be some with whom we establish an especially close bond. Such friendships are important, not first and foremost as a means to emotional fulfilment, but as a matter of wisdom. We need good friends if we are to avoid making a mess of our lives and instead 'run with perseverance the race marked out for us' (Hebrews 12:1). That is true of all of us, whoever we are: male or female, married or single, extroverts or introverts.

MEN AND WOMEN

Generalizations are always risky, but it does seem that women are often more consciously relational than men. They can be quicker to recognize their need for friendship and put more effort into it. Men tend to be more task-orientated, to such an extent that many can work alongside colleagues for years without ever having a personal conversation. Women usually talk when they meet, whereas men are often happier doing things together. Both sexes need to be encouraged to go beyond the superficial in conversation, but that is often a greater challenge for men.

Men are not helped to form deeper friendships by the widespread social expectation that they should be self-reliant. James Wagenvoord, in a book designed to help women understand men, describes the pressure:

He shall not cry. He shall not display weakness. He shall not need affection or gentleness or warmth. He shall comfort but not desire comforting. He shall be needed but not need. He shall touch

but not be touched. He shall be steel not flesh.
He shall be inviolate in his manhood. He shall
stand alone.[3]

Unless men are able to resist this unhelpful understanding of masculinity and be able to be vulnerable with each another, they will always have companions, but not friends.

MARRIED AND SINGLE

When a colleague of mine retired some years ago, she thanked her friends in her farewell speech and remarked: 'For those of us who are single, our friends are our lifeline.' I know what she means, as do most single people. In the absence of an exclusive romantic partnership, we are especially conscious of our need to find intimacy in a variety of other relationships. It is important, however, that married people also recognize their need for close friendships. To rely on just one other person for encouragement, wisdom and support, places a huge burden on them which they will not be able to fulfil. It is important that couples do not allow their friendships to fall into disrepair, not only so that they can be a support to others, but also for their own good. There will be times, for example, when they need to turn to someone else because their partner is not around or, in a particular situation, is not in a position to help. Wisdom suggests that this should almost always be someone of the same sex. Healthy Christian marriages do not have an exclusively inward focus, but are fuelled by looking up to Christ and strengthened by looking out to others, both to give and receive.

ALL PERSONALITY TYPES

We are dependent creatures with a built-in need to rely both on God and one another. That truth will be a particular challenge to those who are naturally quieter and more self-contained. Do not believe the lie that you need not make the effort to get out of your shell and interact deeply with others. None of us is exempt; we may differ in being more gregarious or more reserved, but all of us are united, as human beings made in God's image, in our need for intimate relationship.

Some people relate almost exclusively by caring for others and seeking to fix them. We find our identity in our role as leader or pastor, and can even convince ourselves that whereas others are weak and need helping, we are strong and independent and do not need anyone to get close to us. We may be nervous of such intimacy, as it would involve the risk of the mask slipping and our own weakness being revealed, but it is vital if we are to avoid having only followers but few, if any, of the friends we all need in living the Christian life. It is important, therefore, that we resist our desire to be seen as always strong and in control. Even the Lord Jesus in the Garden of Gethsemane acknowledged his need of friends to stand with him in that time of great trial, and lamented the fact that they did not. We too must be prepared to recognize our own need of friendships, so that those of us who lead are not just ahead or above others, but also alongside them. If that is to happen, we must accept that we will not be able to lead in every situation or always have the last word. There are no exceptions; we all need friends.

QUESTIONS FOR REFLECTION & DISCUSSION

- How is the theme of friendship related to the gospel?

- Why is friendship essential to:

    our humanity?

    living wisely?

- Are our closest friendships 'carnal', 'worldly' or 'spiritual'?

- What more could we do to cultivate spiritual friendships?

- Is it true that men face particular challenges in making deeper friendships?

- What particular challenges do women face?

- How does being married or single affect our friendships?

- What impact does our personality have on our friendships?

TRUE FRIENDSHIP IS CLOSE

2

'A FRIEND WHO STICKS CLOSER THAN A BROTHER'

A man of many companions may come to ruin, but there is a friend who sticks closer than a brother. (Proverbs 18:24)

Family bonds were very important in the ancient world, and yet a bond can be established between friends which goes so deep that the friend can be relied on even more than family. The implication of the proverb is that we should strive to forge such friendships, rather than surround ourselves only with companions who may be good company, but who do not really know us and on whom, if the crunch comes, we cannot rely. That leads to an uncomfortable question: have we got such friends?

CHALLENGES TO FRIENDSHIP

No doubt every generation has experienced an

unfulfilled longing for intimacy, but it is surely greater today, not least because so many pressures conspire to make the forging and keeping of friendships harder than it has been before.

One factor has been our increased mobility. My parents have lived in homes within a five mile radius since they were married in 1961, and my father remained in the same job for over forty years. That settled existence has helped provide them with a large group of friends, many of whom they have known for decades. Such continuity is rare these days, with many moving from job to job and place to place throughout their lives. Increasing numbers live in cities, which often provide an experience of 'proximity without community'.[1] People are packed in close to each other in public transport systems and apartment blocks, and yet often remain lost and anonymous within the surging crowds.

Advances in technology can certainly bring relational benefits, but they have also led to an increase in isolation. We have too often allowed gadgets to take the place of deeper communication with other human beings, rather than to assist it. One computer game was advertised with the words: 'Not got any friends? Don't worry – with this game you won't need any'.[2]

Sadly, there are some for whom the television or computer screen is their best friend: they know the residents of Albert Square or Coronation Street better than their own neighbours, and are more emotionally engaged with the characters in a game than with the people they meet in real life; they have the illusion of social interaction without the reality. We are in danger of raising a generation that finds it hard to relate to others because it has so little experience of doing so.

'FRIENDING' AND 'FRIENDSHIP'

When used well, modern forms of communication can be great tools in sustaining close friendships, so that we can be in regular contact even when we are far apart. Without care, however, we will find that we are simply adding an ever-increasing number to our list of companions without ever really getting to know them. Joanne Harris, who wrote the novel *Chocolat*, was so concerned about the effect the Internet was having on her relationships that she stopped using it completely. She had noticed that the hours she spent communicating online with a long list of people she hardly knew meant she never had time to see any of her close friends. 'Even for someone, like myself, who ought to know better,' she wrote, 'a virtual hug from a stranger can sweeten an otherwise bad day. It's all too easy to forget that this is an illusion; a false intimacy that serves only to compensate for the absence of a real one.'[3]

We need to recognize that there is a difference between 'friending' – relationships which are conducted almost exclusively in cyberspace – and friendship. In friending, more is always better; but in friendship it is quality, not quantity, that matters. Our Facebook profile might tell us that we have 464 friends, but how many really know us? How many would we be willing to make real sacrifices for? How many are there on whom we can rely in times of need? If we just have companions, but very few, or no, real friends, we are heading for trouble. So we must ask that uncomfortable question again: have we got such friends?

FRIENDSHIP IN MARRIAGE

One context in which we should expect to find close friendship is marriage. Marriage is certainly more than friendship, but it should not be less. A spouse should be not just a lover, but a best friend. That will demand time and effort, as a couple seek to support one another in their shared life together. If we are hoping to marry we should be looking, above all, not for the perfect partner for romantic dates, but for a friend who can travel with us through all of life. For Christians, that must therefore mean someone who is on the same path, seeking to follow Christ. This may require a complete rethink about our priorities for a future partner. Tim and Kathy Keller express it well:

What, then, is marriage for? It is for helping each other to become our future glory-selves, the new creations that God will eventually make us. The common horizon husband and wife look toward is the Throne, and the holy, spotless and blameless nature we will have. I can think of no more powerful common horizon than that, and that is why putting a Christian friendship at the heart of a marriage relationship can lift it to a level that no other vision of marriage approaches … We think of a prospective spouse as primarily a lover (or a provider), and if he or she can be a friend on top of that, well isn't that nice! We should be going at it the other way around. Screen first for friendship. Look for someone who understands you better than you do yourself, who makes you a better person just by being around them. And then explore whether that friendship could become a romance and a marriage. So many people go about their dating starting from the wrong end, and they end up in marriages that aren't really about anything and aren't going anywhere.[4]

DIFFERENCES BETWEEN MARRIAGE AND FRIENDSHIP

At a time when the meaning of marriage is being redefined by society, we need to understand the differences between marriage and friendship. Marriage is the exclusive, covenantal commitment of a man and a woman for life. The Bible teaches that sexual intercourse, which is designed to express and strengthen that covenant, should only take place in that context. Friendship should not seek to copy marriage by either demanding exclusive commitment or containing sexual expression. We are free to develop deep friendships, which can be a great blessing, as long as these boundaries are not crossed. Our society's obsession with sex and its assumption that any especially close relationship, even between people of the same gender, may have a sexual element to it, whether acted on or not, has sadly raised suspicions about such friendships. We should not be intimidated by these pressures, while also avoiding naivety. Care and wisdom will especially be needed if we are conscious that sexual feelings are aroused in a friendship.

THE IDOLATRY OF EROS

Having recognized the vital importance of marriage, and of friendship as a vital ingredient within it, I want to sound a warning note, which I touched on in the previous chapter. It has been strikingly expressed by Andrew Sullivan, who has written: 'the great modern enemy of friendship has turned out to be love'.[5] By 'love' he does not mean the care and concern for others which is essential to friendship, but rather what he calls 'the idolatry of Eros': the belief that true intimacy can only be found in the romantic sexual union of a couple.

The Bible certainly has a very high view of marriage, but it is not designed to bear the weight that is placed on it when a husband and wife expect all their relational needs to be met by one another. The result is that they not only put impossible burdens on each other, but also give insufficient attention to other friendships. Single people suffer from the same delusion, too often believing the lie that they are bound to experience miserable, isolated lives unless they can find a spouse. In their commendable desire to protect marriage and the family from contemporary challenges, churches can unwittingly become part of the problem by giving the impression that romantic love is an essential ingredient to human flourishing. Let us certainly keep promoting marriage but, as we do so, let's not forget the great emphasis the Bible also places on friendship.

'WE HAPPY FEW'

Marriage is the closest human relationship, but it should not be the only context in which we experience intimacy. Amongst our larger group of friends we should aim to have a small group with whom we share life at a deeper level over the longer term. These are the equivalent of David's 'mighty men' (2 Samuel 23:8) or the 'happy few', the 'band of brothers' of Shakespeare's *Henry V*.[6] The Lord Jesus chose twelve disciples to whom he related more deeply than with others. It seems he was especially close to three of them, Peter, James and John (see Mark 9:2), and with John in particular – 'the disciple whom Jesus loved' (John 13:23). The apostle Paul also had an inner circle of friends such as Timothy, whom he called 'my dear son' (2 Timothy 1:2) and Luke, whom he described as 'our dear friend' (Colossians 4:14).

In developing close friendships we should beware the danger of cliquey exclusivity, which can hurt the feelings of others. This requires sensitivity in recognizing, for example, that coffee after church is not the ideal regular time for intense conversations that only include a few. Once again, Jesus is a perfect model for us in the way in which he related to many in a crowd and usually reserved his closer interactions with his disciples to private moments.

THE GREATER GAIN OF FAITHFULNESS TO CHRIST

Committed long-term friendships are an important witness to the possibility of real intimacy and relational security outside, or alongside, marriage. Our culture, with its low view of friendship, doubts that this is possible and, for that reason, believes that churches which urge members to uphold the Bible's teaching and remain celibate, rather than enter a same-sex partnership or a marriage with a non-Christian, are condemning them to a life of unsustainable isolation. That must not and need not be so. Those who face unwanted singleness will experience the pain of an unfulfilled longing for an exclusive sexual relationship with one special person for life, which the Bible reserves for the marriage of a man and a woman, but they need not feel isolated. There may be a loss in being faithful to Christ, but he promises that it will be exceeded by an even greater gain:

'I tell you the truth,' Jesus replied, 'no-one who has left home or brothers or sisters or mother or father or children or fields for me and the gospel will fail to receive a hundred times as much in this present age (homes, brothers, sisters, mothers, children and fields – and with them, persecutions) and in the age to come, eternal life.' (Mark 10:29–30)

Although I feel that I have made very few significant sacrifices as a Christian, I can certainly testify from my own experience that, as Christ promised, they have been more than compensated by his gracious provision. Alongside a wonderful family, I am especially grateful for a superb church family who love me and pray for me, as well as many good friends. Although there are challenges in being single, one of the greatest advantages is the extra time available to invest in friendships, which bring much joy and strengthen me in living for Christ.

'OH MY FRIENDS, THERE IS NO FRIEND'

Rather as the ancient mariner lamented that there was 'Water, water, everywhere, Nor any drop to drink,'[7] Aristotle is once reported to have exclaimed, 'Oh my friends, there is no friend.' What if we recognize the same reality: that we have many 'friends' who are just companions, but a lack of real friends who know us deeply? In this situation we should be both discerning and deliberate.

a) Be discerning

Those who are lonely and feel isolated are in danger of rushing into any friendship that is available without thinking about the possible consequences. C.S. Lewis observes, 'Friendship can be a school of virtue, but also a school of vice. It is ambivalent. It makes good men better and bad men worse.'[8] Proverbs 13:20 expresses the same truth: 'He who walks with the wise grows wise, but a companion of fools suffers harm.' Parents understand that, which is why, when their teenagers go out, they ask not just 'Where are you going?' or 'When will you be back?' but also, most importantly, 'Who are you going with?'

Some of us may have plenty of friends, but they are the wrong ones. Far from helping us live as we should, they lead us astray. Wisdom may therefore require not just the making of friendships but, in some cases, the breaking of them – or, at least, the loosening of certain ties. It is good to have a range of friendships, but our closest should be with those who share our highest goals and help us live up to them.

b) Be deliberate

Friendship does not occur by accident, but requires time and effort. As Hugh Black writes:

the commonest mistake is that we spread our intercourse over a mass and have no depth of heart left. We lament that we have no staunch and faithful friend when we have not really expended the love which produces such. We want to reap where we have not sown ... The secret of friendship is just the secret of all spiritual blessings; the way to get is to give.[9]

In other words, the way to have good friends is to *be* a good friend. Instead of lamenting that no one invites us for a meal, that our church is so unfriendly and that everyone relates at such a superficial level, let us take the initiative to open our homes and lives and see what happens.

QUESTIONS FOR REFLECTION & DISCUSSION

- What are the challenges to friendship that you experience?

- How can we ensure that our use of technology helps, rather than hinders, our desire to form close friendships?

- What implications will there be for a marriage, or a search for a spouse, if married couples should be best friends?

- How is 'the idolatry of Eros' an enemy of friendship for both married and single people?

- What can we do to ensure that church really is a family, so that nobody feels isolated as a follower of Christ?

- Are there some friendships that are harmful to us? What should we do about this?

- What can we do if we find that we have many companions, but very few, if any, real friends?

TRUE FRIENDSHIP IS CONSTANT

3

'A FRIEND LOVES AT ALL TIMES'

It is often remarked by those who have experienced a time of real difficulty that it has shown them who their true friends are. As Proverbs points out, superficial friends soon fade away:

Wealth brings many friends, but a poor man's friend deserts him. (Proverbs 19:4)

A poor man is shunned by all his relatives – how much more do his friends avoid him! Though he pursues them with pleading, they are nowhere to be found. (Proverbs 19:7)

Real friends, by contrast, stick with us through thick and thin: 'A friend loves at all times, and a brother is born for adversity' (Proverbs 17:17). There is no better example of this in the Bible than Jonathan's love for David. Even though his father, Saul, had turned against David and was determined to kill him, Jonathan remained steadfastly loyal. After he died, David mourned deeply: 'I grieve for you, Jonathan my brother; you were very dear to me. Your love for me was wonderful, more wonderful than that of women' (2 Samuel 1:26).

WHAT KIND OF FRIEND AM I?

When thinking about Jonathan's moving example, there is a danger that we will compare him with our friends and lament that they are not offering the support we feel we need. But, rather than think about others, we should face the challenge ourselves and ask, 'What kind of friend am I?' There is a danger that we can be so wrapped up in our own lives that we have no time or energy left for others, even at a time of crisis – when they are afflicted, for example, by ill health, bereavement or relational difficulties. As a result, we resent any sacrifice that may be demanded of us, keep our heads down and do the bare minimum.

Perhaps we are confident that if a friend was truly in need, we would be there for them. But would anyone think of turning to us in such circumstances? Have we kept our friendships in good shape in better times so that they are prepared for the moment when a crisis occurs?

A few years ago, I came to the uncomfortable realization that the answer to that question in my case was probably 'no'. I had made many friendships over the years, but maintaining them had not been a priority. I allowed myself to become so busy that I hardly saw old friends and contented myself with an occasional group email to let them know what I was up to. It was hardly surprising, therefore, that when I became conscious of the need to rely more deeply on friends myself, it was not immediately obvious who to turn to. I was reminded during a sabbatical of a truth that I knew in my head, but had hardly allowed to impact my heart and actions: that nothing was more important than relationships, with God and with others, and that I needed to reorder my life accordingly. I have tried since then, not always successfully, to prioritize time for friendships.

FRIENDSHIPS MUST BE MAINTAINED

Wisdom says, 'Do not forsake your friend and the friend of your father' (Proverbs 27:10). Friendships must not only be made, but also maintained. It is, of course, not always possible to do this. I had many friends in my school days, but only keep in regular contact with two of them. I am pleased if I happen to meet others, but I do not feel guilty about not seeing them often.

There are different circles of friendship and it is inevitable that some who once were in the inner circle move, over time, into one of the outer circles as we see less of them. As this happens, we must be careful that the inner circle does not gradually empty altogether, but instead ensure that we keep a few of the old friendships in good repair, as well as forming new ones. This may well need conscious effort as we get older.

I remember as a student seeing an advert for a seminar on friendship at a conference, and wondering which sad people would sign up for it. Until then I had always been surrounded by people of my own age, all of whom were single with plenty of spare time and, in that context, I formed friendships naturally. That is not the experience of all younger people, but many do find that friendship gets more difficult as life goes on. I gradually discovered that the deep relationships of my early life could not be automatically sustained without any conscious effort on my part and that, as life became busier, I needed to put time aside to maintain them, while also developing newer friendships.

STRENGTHENING FRIENDSHIPS

It is time now to ask what practical steps we could take if we are conscious, as I was, that our friendships have fallen into disrepair and need to be strengthened, so that they become both close and constant. There is no magic formula that will guarantee strong friendships, but here are some suggestions from what I have observed in others and have sought to apply myself.

a) Be selective

This first suggestion might sound rather cold and calculating, but the reality is that we simply cannot invest the same amount of time and attention in every relationship that we have. Some of us will have no difficulty in knowing who our closest friends are, but others will have to make a deliberate decision to prioritize certain friendships. That does not mean ignoring the others, but it will involve doing all we can to ensure we are sharing life at a deeper level with some.

b) Be open

If we want greater intimacy with others, we will have to be prepared to be open with them. That may involve sharing our hopes, fears and passions, as well as our darkest secrets or greatest temptations.

I have found time and again that as I have taken the risk of being open with trusted friends, far from recoiling from me in horror, they have responded by revealing some of their own struggles, and our friendship has deepened.

c) Be interested

We all want someone to listen to us, but are we prepared to listen to others and take a real interest in their lives? Friendships are often strengthened by good questions. Many will be fairly mundane such as 'How has your day been?' or 'What are you up to over the summer?', but to avoid superficiality, we will need to go deeper at times. We should show an interest not just in what our friends are doing, but in how they are thinking and feeling. And let us not forget to ask about their Christian lives. Good questions might include 'What have you been learning from God's word recently?' or 'How can I pray for you?' A regular meeting with one or two others to pray can be an excellent context in which to ask such questions and to develop stronger friendships.

d) Be committed

Friendships grow as we express love in the three areas listed by John Frame as allegiance, affection and action.[1] Couples have an opportunity to demonstrate these when they choose people for whom they have the deepest affection and allegiance as maid of honour, bridesmaids, best man and ushers at their wedding or as godparents for their children. Single people can find it hard to know where it is appropriate to direct their love and how to express it. In the words of a character in the film *Magnolia*, 'I really do have love to give; I just don't know where to put it.' It may be we simply have to decide to invest a greater amount of effort in certain friendships and see what happens.

There is a place for declarations of commitment and love, but these qualities will often develop naturally as we demonstrate them by our actions. Rather than waiting for others to take the initiative, we can do so ourselves in countless ways, whether we are single or married, not least by prioritizing time to see friends. Given the many demands on us, that might require making a regular commitment, rather than simply waiting for a moment when we are both free, which may happen rarely. I have appreciated enormously the kindness of two families in inviting me to share a weekly meal with them. Monday supper and Wednesday breakfast are relational highlights which I always look forward to, however hectic the rest of the week may be.

The best friendships have often been expressed and strengthened through relatively insignificant actions, such as listening to dreams and concerns, writing a note before an exam, giving a lift to hospital or looking after children for the afternoon. It is often like this, through countless small actions which are then reciprocated in other ways, that close friendships develop over time and grow in both affection and allegiance. Then, as Hugh Black writes: 'Through little occasions of helpfulness, we are training for the great trial, should it ever come, when the fabric of friendship will be tested to the very foundation.'[2]

WHEN FRIENDSHIPS FACE TENSION

All relationships between sinful human beings are bound to experience tension at times. The closer the friendship, the deeper the pain that is likely to be felt when one believes they have been let down or betrayed by the other. If we are at fault ourselves, even if only in part, we should be quick to apologize and do all we can to put things right. As Hugh Black rightly comments: 'Our brother may be so offended that he is harder won than a strong city, but he is far more worth winning; and even if the effort be unsuccessful, it is better than the cowardice that suffers a bloodless defeat.'[3]

If we feel ourselves to have been wronged, it is important that our reaction is driven by grace and wisdom, rather than emotion. If an apology is offered, it should be accepted without recrimination or the bearing of any grudge. Some offences, however much they may hurt, are too trivial to dwell on. If so, it may be that our response needs to focus on ourselves and why we have reacted in such an exaggerated way, rather than on the other person.

Other wrongs may be more serious, in which case the teaching of Jesus in Matthew 18 may apply. The principle is to avoid stirring things up by complaining to others, but rather to keep the matter as private as possible: 'If your brother sins against you, go and show him his fault, just between the two of you. If he listens to you, you have won your brother over' (Matthew 18:15).

It can be especially difficult when fault is not acknowledged or when two friends are hurt, but both feel the other is to blame. Talking can help to clear up misunderstandings, but sometimes the different perspectives remain and threaten to cause a lasting breach in the relationship. In such circumstances we should do all we can to bring healing, both in our attitude and actions, which may mean determining to move on and leave the dispute behind. Intimacy may have been damaged, but it can be rebuilt over time. That will, of course, require the participation of both parties. All we can do is resolve to be gracious and loving in our own behaviour. If our friend does not reciprocate, we may have to come to a sad acceptance that, for the time being at least, we are no longer able to relate as before.

THE NEED FOR PATIENCE

Aristotle was surely right when he observed: 'The desire for friendship comes quickly. Friendship does not.' There is no short cut to intimacy; it requires commitment over the long haul. That may be frustrating, but the rewards are well worth it. Those who have been blessed with friends who have remained faithful for years, or even decades, know the pleasure and security they bring. It is worth stressing once again that we must not wait until others relate like this to us. The way to have such constant friends is to *be* a constant friend.

QUESTIONS FOR REFLECTION & DISCUSSION

- Have we experienced friendships going cold by neglect?

    What has gone wrong?

    What could we do differently in the future?

- What have we appreciated in the way others have shown friendship in allegiance, affection and action towards us? What can we learn from their example?

- What responses should we seek to avoid when a friendship faces tension? What will a gracious reaction look like?

TRUE FRIENDSHIP IS CANDID

4

WHO ARE THEIR FRIENDS?

The leaders of one church I know always ask each other after a pastoral crisis has emerged, 'Who are their friends?' Who was there to help before the situation deteriorated so badly? Very often the answer is 'no one'; nobody was allowed close enough to know what was really going on, so the marriage difficulties, temptations or anxieties were faced in isolation. They might have been addressed, or at least diminished, if only others had been involved sooner. At the very least, the pain of the situation could have been lessened, if it had been shared.

As we saw in the previous chapter, if we are to develop true friendship with others we must be prepared to be open with them. The apostle Paul commands Christians to 'rejoice with those who rejoice' and 'mourn with those who mourn' (Romans

12:15), but that is impossible unless we know what joys and sadnesses others are experiencing. Too often, even in churches, we struggle to get beyond superficial interactions. Paul Tripp's words are uncomfortably close to the experience of many:

[W]e live in interwoven networks of terminally casual relationships. We live with the delusion that we know one another, but we really don't. We call our easygoing, self-protective, and often theologically platitudinous conversations 'fellowship,' but they seldom ever reach the threshold of true fellowship. We know cold demographic details about one another (married or single, type of job, number of kids, general location of housing, etc.), but we know little about the struggle of faith that is waged every day behind well-maintained personal boundaries. One of the things that still shocks me in counselling, even after all these years, is how little I often know about people I have counted as true friends. I can't tell you how many times, in talking with friends who have come to me for help, that I have been hit with details of difficulty and struggle far beyond anything I would have predicted. Privatism is not just practiced by the lonely unbeliever; it is rampant in the church as well.[1]

GETTING BEHIND THE MASK

We are often reluctant to be more self-revealing with other people because of a perception that they have their lives completely under control and that they would be horrified if they really knew what was going on behind the mask of our similarly sorted exterior. But the Bible is clear that we are all, by nature, deeply flawed individuals living in a broken world, so we will all, in our different ways, be facing battles against difficult circumstances and besetting sins. The greater our understanding of the Bible's teaching about the depth of human sin, the less we are likely to be shocked by the revelations of our friends' struggles, and the more we will be willing to be open with them about our own.

From time to time a friend has said to me: 'Vaughan, I recognize my need for accountability, so I want you to feel free to ask me any question you like.' That is not as helpful as it sounds. If I say, 'Are you being completely honest when you fill in your tax return?' he might be deeply offended, but how am I to know that is not a temptation for him when it is for plenty of other Christians? It is much more helpful if I not only have permission to ask questions, but am also told what questions they should be. What are the areas of particular difficulty? One way I help people try to discern their special points of vulnerability is to ask, 'If you were the devil, where would you direct your attack against yourself?'

'FAITHFUL ARE THE WOUNDS OF A FRIEND'

If true intimacy is to develop, we must be willing to be honest in talking to our friends not only about our own failings but also, when appropriate, about theirs. Very often it is love for myself and a fear of being badly received, rather than a love for my friend, that holds me back from speaking an uncomfortable truth to him. But if I only praise him and never point out any faults, I am certainly not helping him: 'Whoever flatters his neighbours is spreading a net for his feet' (Proverbs 29:5). If our friends are forever telling us how wonderful we are and never pointing out our weaknesses, which they, more than anyone, are in a position to see, they are setting a trap for us.

It is painful to watch some of the *X Factor* auditions. You fear the worst when the candidate is asked what her dream is and replies confidently that she wants to be the next Shirley Bassey or Beyoncé. She then sings without hitting a note, apparently undeterred by the giggling of the judges. Some try to be kind and suggest that 'Perhaps singing isn't for you', but there is always one who says what we are all thinking: 'Do you realize you sound like a cat wailing?' That prompts a furious reaction: 'You don't know what you are talking about. I'm a brilliant singer; I'm going to make it to the top and then you'll be sorry!' How could she be so deluded? The answer is revealed when she leaves the room to be comforted by friends and family, who all assure her that she has a wonderful voice and a brilliant future, whatever the panel says. They think they are being kind, but they are destroying her life with their lies.

If I asked a group of church members to describe their pastor's greatest weaknesses they would all probably say much the same thing, but very often the pastor is completely unaware of the issues mentioned, because no one has ever told them. I am certainly not suggesting that you should take it upon yourself to put this right; it is very likely not your place to do so. The point is simply that there must be some who are able to speak to us about areas in our lives where growth is needed. The more powerful or influential we are, the more likely it is that our failings will remain unmentioned and unaddressed. If we are unable to think of anyone who is prepared to speak to us in this way, we should do something about it. If we are wise, we will understand the value of loving candour:

Better is open rebuke than hidden love. Wounds from a friend can be trusted, but an enemy multiplies kisses. (Proverbs 27:5–6)

As we will see in the next chapter, the tongue is a powerful weapon and should be used with great care, but there are times when our friends should use it even when it hurts us. There is truth in Oscar Wilde's witticism: 'A true friend stabs you in the front'. As Ralph Waldo Emerson put it: 'It is better to be the thorn in the side of your friend than his echo.'

RESPONDING TO CRITICISM

Could it be that the reason why there is no one who feels able to challenge or disagree with us is that we will not let them? Perhaps they have tried in the past and we have responded by being over-defensive or deflecting the criticism back to them, accusing them of being disloyal or insensitive. If so, they would have learnt not to do the same again and, as a result, a barrier to intimacy has been established in our relationship.

It is vital that we learn to respond well to criticism from wherever it comes, and especially from those who love us, if we are to mature as people. One friend of mine suggests a three-point approach to criticism:

- Expect it: given our sins and weaknesses, we should be surprised we receive so little criticism.

- Examine it: we should resist the instinctive temptation to defend ourselves or attack the critic, but rather consider whether there is truth in what is being said.

- Endure it: even when we feel it is unfair, we must not be resentful.[2]

BECOMING 'BETTER THAN MYSELF'

Gordon MacDonald expresses well the true goal of Christian friendship:

*There is a certain 'niceness' to a friendship where I can be, as they say, **myself**. But what I really need are relationships in which I will be encouraged to become **better than** myself. **Myself** needs to grow a little each day. I don't want to be the **myself** I was yesterday. I want to be the **myself** that is developing each day to be more of a Christlike person.[3]*

That goal will require occasional criticisms from my friends, but their loving candour demands more than that. Sometimes what I need is honest, impartial advice which flows from a loving concern, not, first and foremost, for my happiness, but rather for my holiness and wholehearted discipleship. It may not always be what I want to hear, but I know it is motivated by a desire that I become the best I can be for Christ. Such wisdom is worth its weight in gold: 'Perfume and incense bring joy to the heart, and the pleasantness of one's friend springs from his earnest counsel' (Proverbs 27:9).

SPEAKING THE TRUTH IN LOVE

Above all, what we need from our friends is the application of the gospel to our lives. The ministry of God's word is not limited to those with public responsibility for preaching and teaching in our churches, but is shared by all of us. We are to 'teach and admonish *one another* with all wisdom' (Colossians 3:16, my italics). As we seek to be helpful to our friends, we need to ask how we can bring the gospel to bear on their lives. The answer is unlikely to be complicated and they should probably have been able to work it out for themselves, but they still need others to help them to hear, believe and apply it; we all do.

It is very rare that I require experts in psychology or pastoral counselling to work out what I need to hear. More often than not, I just need friends who will point me to what I already know well, but find hard to truly accept and live by. That will mean frequent reminders of the amazing grace of God revealed in the gospel of Christ. That wonderful message always brings me hope, no matter how dire my circumstances or how deep my sin. I am a much-loved child of God, completely accepted by him and able to call him my Father because of Christ's death for me. I have received the Holy Spirit and am a new person with a new power within, so I do not have to be trapped by destructive patterns of thinking or behaviour. As friends walk together through life, 'speaking the truth in love', they can expect real and lasting change as they 'grow up into him who is the head, that is, Christ' (Ephesians 4:15).

- What hinders openness in friendship?

- Is there anyone who feels able to speak hard truths to us? If not, what can we do about that?

- How do we tend to respond to criticism? How could we improve?

- How could we be better at applying the gospel to our friends' lives?

TRUE FRIENDSHIP IS CAREFUL

5

THE POWER OF THE TONGUE

I was once told that the tongue weighs about 0.4 per cent of our total body weight. I cannot think of a painless way of checking that claim, so I am prepared to accept it. Yet, despite its small size, the tongue has enormous power for good or ill: 'The tongue has the power of life and death' (Proverbs 18:21). It may only be 3 inches long, but it can fell a man 6 foot tall, at least metaphorically, and then lift him up again. Given its power, we should exercise great sensitivity in how we use our tongues, not least with regard to our friends. True friendship will sometimes be candid, but it must always be careful.

Proverbs encourages us to listen before we open our mouth: 'He who answers before listening – that is his folly and his shame' (Proverbs 18:13). Sometimes our friends are not looking to us for any particular advice; they only want someone to listen. They can be helped simply by verbalizing their dilemma. Just hearing themselves expressing their thoughts and feelings can enable them to see where they are being foolish or how they should respond to their situation. Even when there is no obvious solution for us to offer, it can be a help to them just to know that someone else understands what they are going through.

Having listened, we should stop to think before saying anything: 'The heart of the righteous weighs its answers, but the mouth of the wicked gushes evil' (Proverbs 15:28). That applies to the words we write, as well as those we say. When words are written down, the impact can be multiplied because their message is repeated over and over again from the page or computer screen. Words of encouragement, especially in a letter or card, can be a significant boost, but written words can also bring lasting damage.

In the days when we wrote more letters, there were various helpful stages that slowed down the process: putting it into the envelope, finding the address, sticking on a stamp and then walking to the letter box. That gave time to consider whether it was really wise to send those words. Even then, I was advised always to sleep on it before posting a letter which contained any complaint or criticism. There are no such protections when we communicate electronically, so we need to make sure that before pressing the send button we ask: 'Is this true?', 'Is it necessary?', 'Is it kind?' If the answer to any of those questions is 'no', then we should not say it and must not send it.

NO PLACE FOR GOSSIP

There is certainly no place for gossip in friendship:

A perverse man stirs up dissension, and a gossip separates close friends. (Proverbs 16:28)

He who covers over an offence promotes love, but whoever repeats the matter separates close friends. (Proverbs 17:9)

A gossip betrays a confidence; so avoid a man who talks too much. (Proverbs 20:19)

If a friend does me the honour of opening up to me about something very private and personal, my lips must be sealed. Too often we break confidences in subtle ways by hinting at some information we are privy to, saying, for example, 'I can't say much, but between you and me, there are issues with Jane.' We may feel that we have given no secrets away, but the context of the conversation makes it clear what we mean. Once others discover that we are not able to keep our mouths shut in this way, they will make sure they do not share anything significant with us, and we will find it much harder to develop closer friendships.

REMOVING A SPECK

As we saw in the last chapter, there are times when love demands that we should mention a friend's fault, but that must always be done with great humility. If we point out the speck in our brother's eye, we should do so with full awareness of the plank in our own (Matthew 7:3). And we should not use the verbal equivalent of a hammer to remove it, but rather do so with the sensitivity and love which gives our intervention the greatest chance of having the desired effect. It may then do much good: 'Like an ear-ring of gold or an ornament of fine gold is a wise man's rebuke to a listening ear' (Proverbs 25:12).

My former boss, David Fletcher, was a wonderful model of gentle rebuking. Despite my youth and lack of experience in pastoral ministry, I was always quick to offer my opinion about what he should do as rector of St Ebbe's. He bore this with amazing patience before one day saying to me, 'You know,

Vaughan, that I love you very much. In fact, I love and admire you so much that when I write my autobiography, I am going to call it *Curates I Have Served Under*'. I walked away from the conversation feeling rather flattered before the penny dropped and the subtle rebuke began to sink in. I hope it had an effect. The way it was so graciously administered gave it the best chance of doing so.

THE NEED FOR EMOTIONAL SENSITIVITY

As friends, we will need the emotional sensitivity to discern the right thing to say at the right time and in the right way. Even kind words will not be received well when they are delivered too loudly over breakfast if the recipient is not a morning person: 'If a man loudly blesses his neighbour early in the morning, it will be taken as a curse' (Proverbs 27:14). And if a friend is feeling low, do not bombard them with cheerfulness: 'Like one who takes away a garment on a cold day … is one who sings songs to a heavy heart' (Proverbs 25:20). We need to learn the effect our words and actions are likely to have on others and adapt accordingly, so as to avoid blundering through life, however well-meaning, causing offence and upset wherever we go. That will involve understanding the differences between our friends. Some will need banter and jokes to lift their spirits, while others will just want us to sit quietly with them when they are low. One may be so thick skinned that we would need to be very blunt with them to get any critical point across, while another might be sensitive and so demand careful handling.

KNOWING THE BOUNDARIES

I have an excessive fear of being a burden on others, which can be an obstacle to intimacy. I always assume I will be in the way if I call around uninvited, but I need to believe my friends when they say that they really would like me to do so and would love to see me more. I need to heed the advice of a Scandinavian proverb: 'Go often to the house of your friends; for weeds soon choke the unused path.' Others are in the danger of going in the opposite direction and should listen to Proverbs 25:17: 'Seldom set foot in your neighbour's house – too much of you, and he will hate you.'

We should recognize that a change of circumstances may mean that it is no longer appropriate for us to expect as much time with a friend as before. That is especially so when they have got married. Marriage should certainly not bring an end to other friendships, but it is likely to change them. A single man has told me that he and his married friend work on the principle that a good friendship strengthens a marriage, while a bad one weakens it. They aim to arrange their friendship in such a way that the wife is grateful, rather than resentful, for any time he spends with his friend, because he comes back a better husband and father.

EMOTIONAL DEPENDENCY

We must be on our guard against any form of jealousy in our relationships. Jealousy often hides behind other emotions and seeks to justify itself by finding fault with someone else. We should make every effort to unmask and resist it, recognizing that, as Hugh Black says, it 'is usually the fruit, not of love, but of self-love'.[1]

Jealousy can be one sign that a relationship has degenerated into a destructive emotional dependency. This is defined by Lori Rentzel in her booklet on the subject as the state which 'occurs when the ongoing presence and nurturing of another is believed to be necessary for personal security'. She helpfully unpacks some of the differences between a healthy friendship and an emotionally dependent one:

A healthy friendship is free and generous. Both friends are eager to include others in their activities. They are happy when one friend hits it off with another person. In a good friendship we desire to see the other reach his or her full potential, developing new interests and skills. In healthy relationships we are affected by the things our friends say and do, but our reactions are balanced.

On the other hand, a dependent relationship is ingrown, creating mutual stagnation and limiting personal growth. A casual remark from our friend can send us into the heights of ecstasy or the pits of grief. When a close friend moves away, it is normal for us to feel sorrow and a sense of loss; but if one of the partners in a dependent relationship moves, the other is gripped with anguish, panic and desperation. While healthy friendship is joyful and upbuilding, emotional dependency produces bondage.[2]

When a friendship has become harmful in these kinds of ways, we need to seek help to address the situation. This will require emotional withdrawal, which is likely to be painful, but will be necessary if we and our friend are to allow each other to flourish.

Thankfully, few friendships are spoilt like this, but even in the best friendships we will experience selfishness and frustration, when we feel let down or misunderstood. With this recognition in mind, we need to return to the great theme of the perfect friendship, which only Christ can give us.

- What steps could we take to prevent ourselves from using inappropriate words

    in speech?

    electronically?

- In what situations do we have to be on our guard against gossip?

- How do we decide if we are the right person to point out the fault of another? How can that be done sensitively?

- How can we discern whether we are in contact with our friends too much or too little?

- What are some of the warning signs of an unhelpful emotional dependency? What can we do to avoid it?

TRUE FRIENDSHIP IS CHRIST-CENTRED 6

THE INADEQUACY OF SELF-HELP

I wonder how you have reacted to this book on friendship. As I have reflected on these themes, I have been struck frequently by a profound sense of failure, because I have not been the kind of friend the Bible commends. They have also stirred within me a deep longing: I long to be such a friend and to have such friends.

The self-help books that sell in their millions tell us that we are able to satisfy our relational longings by adopting certain attitudes and taking decisive action. Their advice often begins with an appeal to grow in self-esteem and love for oneself. One author writes: 'When you make friends with yourself you begin a love affair that lasts a lifetime … Self-love is the pre-requisite of loving others.'[1]

The irony is that these books fail to recognize that the solution they offer is the very heart of the problem. Our self-centredness is what destroys our relationships. They cannot be fixed from within, but rather need a deeper love that comes from outside ourselves: the love of God in Christ.

CHRIST FORGIVES OUR GREATEST FAILINGS

God is love and he commands us to be like him. We are to love God with all our heart, soul, mind and strength, and to love our neighbour as ourselves (see Mark 12:30–31), but we have not done this and have instead put self-love first. The results have been disastrous. Even though we long for close relationships with others, we keep spoiling them by our self-centred, thoughtless words and actions. We have let people down and hurt them, perhaps especially those closest to us, and we have also spoilt our relationship with God.

Although God is the loving creator and ruler of everything, by nature we live as if the world belongs to us. He continues to shower us with good gifts, but we take them for granted and hardly, if ever, pause to say thank you. We deserve nothing from him except his judgement for this rebellious ingratitude.

We are quick to turn away from those who hurt us, give them the silent treatment and even look for revenge. God could not be more different. Amazingly, despite our treatment of him, he continues to love us, and is determined to restore our relationship with him. He sent his son Jesus Christ into the world to make that possible.

Jesus always lived in perfect obedience to his heavenly Father and is, therefore, the one person who has ever lived who does not deserve the penalty of separation from him. And yet, that is what he faced on the cross as he received the punishment we deserved. He took our place, so that all who trust in him can be completely forgiven and accepted by God. Jesus himself said, 'Greater love has no-one than this, that he lay down his life for his friends' (John 15:13). Jesus' sacrifice for us was even more wonderful than that, because he died for us when we were still in rebellion against God. As the apostle Paul writes: 'God demonstrates his own love for us in this: While we were still sinners, Christ died for us' (Romans 5:8).

Many of our relationships are insecure because we feel we have to earn the approval and affection of others, and are never quite sure we have done enough. Our relationship with God, by contrast, is completely secure, if we have trusted in Christ, because it depends entirely upon his sacrifice on the cross and not on anything we have done. If you have not turned to Christ, you can do so right now, asking him for forgiveness, and the gift of his Holy Spirit to help you live for him. Those of us who already belong to Christ can thank God again for the amazing free gift of his friendship, which cost him so much.

CHRIST MEETS OUR DEEPEST LONGINGS

As a friend of mine was reaching to pull a history textbook from a high shelf in a library, he dropped it, and as he did so, a piece of paper fell out and fluttered to the floor. He picked it up and read these words, left by a previous reader: 'The Lord Jesus can be as real to you as a human friend.'

We human beings are made as relational creatures in the image of the God, who is love. Above all, we are made to relate to him and, without that relationship, we will always experience emptiness within. People have tried to fill that vacuum with money, pleasure and achievements, but nothing else fits. Not even human relationships, however good they may be, can bring complete fulfilment; only Jesus Christ can ultimately satisfy the hunger of our hearts.

Jesus not only forgives out greatest failings, but also meets our deepest longings. He rose from the dead, is alive and, by the Holy Spirit, can be known today. At the moment, we know him by faith and not by sight (2 Corinthians 5:7). We long for the day when we will see him face to face and know him fully, as we are fully known (1 Corinthians 13:12). Yet, even now, we can have a real relationship with him. As Peter wrote to some Christians in the first century, 'Though you have not seen him, you love him; and even though you do not see him now, you believe in him and are filled with an inexpressible and glorious joy' (1 Peter 1:8).

THE DANGER OF MESSIANIC EXPECTATIONS

Friendships can become destructive if we look to them to take the place that only Christ can fill. Henri Nouwen, who wrote many best-selling books on spirituality, described how this happened after he developed an especially close friendship:

Among my many friends, one had been able to touch me in a way I had never been touched before. Our friendship encouraged me to allow myself to be loved and cared for with greater trust and confidence. It was a totally new experience for me and it brought immense joy and peace. It seemed as if a door of my interior life had been opened, a door that had remained locked during my youth and most of my adult life. But this deeply satisfying friendship became the road to my anguish because soon I discovered that the enormous space that had been opened for me could not be filled by the one who had opened it. I became possessive, needy and dependent, and when the friendship finally had to be interrupted, I fell apart. I felt abandoned, rejected and betrayed.[2]

This experience helped him to see more deeply what he had already understood in his head, but had never really allowed to sink into his heart. He later wrote:

No friend, or lover, no husband or wife, no community or commune will be able to put to rest our deepest cravings for unity and wholeness. And by burdening others with those divine expectations, of which we ourselves are only partially aware, we might inhibit the expression of free friendship and invoke instead feelings of inadequacy and weakness … It is sad to see how sometimes people suffering from loneliness, often deepened by the lack of affection in their immediate family circle, search for a final solution

for their pains and look at a new friend, or a
new lover, or a new community with messianic
expectations.[3]

If we expect anyone other than Christ, whether a
spouse or a friend, to be our saviour, who can meet
our greatest needs and satisfy our deepest longings,
we are bound to be dissatisfied. By looking to that
relationship to bear that much weight, we will
spoil it, or even break it altogether. Our neediness,
and the demands that flow from it, will choke our
friends, rather than allowing them to flourish.
This is the attitude that breeds the diseases that
undermine friendship: emotional manipulation,
control or dependency, jealousy, and demands for
an unhealthy exclusivity. Relationships like that
are selfish and restricting. They are always on edge
with no real security. This is the opposite of the
self-giving, life-enriching friendships that the Bible
portrays. Francis Schaeffer sums up the problem
and points to the solution:

We are finite and therefore we do not expect to
find final sufficiency in any human relationship,
including marriage. The final sufficiency is to be
found only in a relationship with God … If a man
*tries to find **everything** in a man-woman, or a*
friend-friend relationship, he destroys the very

thing he wants and destroys the one he loves. He sucks them dry, he eats them up and they, as well as the relationship are destroyed. But as Christians we do not have to do that. Our sufficiency of relationship is in that which God made it to be, in the infinite-personal God on the basis of the work of Christ in communication and love.[4]

THE GREATEST FRIENDSHIP

The recognition that even the best human friendships are limited is certainly not a reason to avoid them, but is rather a spur to look beyond them to Christ. It is only as our friendships are built on him and all we receive in him that they will have the secure foundation which will enable them truly to flourish. Aelred recognizes this truth in the opening words of his book when he addresses his friend and says, 'Here we are, you and I, and I hope a third, Christ, is in our midst.' He later writes, 'What more sublime can be said of friendship, what more true, what more profitable, than it ought to, and is proved to, begin in Christ, continue in Christ, and be perfected in Christ.'[5]

Only Christ can meet our deepest longings, as he is the greatest friend of all. He is the closest of all friends, who does indeed stick closer than a brother.

By his Holy Spirit he is always with us, wherever we are and whatever we are experiencing. We might be bereaved, divorced, unhappily single or in a difficult marriage, but as Christians we are never alone. We may be facing huge pressures and have no idea which way to turn, but in the midst of the confusion and darkness, Christ is with us. There can be no more constant friend. He has promised his disciples, 'I am with you always' (Matthew 28:20), and God says, 'Never will I leave you; never will I forsake you' (Hebrews 13:5). *Never!* We have often let Christ down, but he is faithful. That certainly does not mean that he turns a blind eye to our faults. He forgives us, but he loves us too much to leave us as we are. He is a candid friend, who shows us where we are wrong and urges us to change, as he often did with his disciples. And he is a careful friend who could not be more gentle: 'A bruised reed he will not break, and a smouldering wick he will not snuff out' (Matthew 12:20).

THE MOST PRECIOUS THING THIS LIFE AFFORDS

The story is told of Shah Abbas of Persia, who was frustrated at his inability to make friends. Whenever he met people, they would bow down to him in respect and fear, so he found it impossible to develop real intimacy with anyone. He therefore decided to take off his royal robes and go to the servants' quarters in disguise to see who he could meet. Right at the bottom of the palace he found the stoker, who kept the fire burning which heated the building. They chatted and got on so well that Abbas continued to go to him over many weeks and they became very close. After a while, he thought it was time to reveal his true identity. 'I am Abbas, your Shah,' he said, 'and you are my friend. So I want to give you anything you ask for, up to half my kingdom.' The stoker replied, 'You have already given me the most precious thing this life affords: your friendship; I ask for nothing more.'

We can rejoice in the parallel story of the amazing love of Christ who left all the glory of heaven to become a servant who was even willing to die for us on the cross. He could not have gone lower than that, and he did it that we might become his friends. If we know him, we already have the most precious thing this life affords. In him we receive complete forgiveness, absolute security as much-loved children of God, and the certain hope of being with him for ever. We will still experience many difficulties in this broken world, but we face them with the most faithful friend imaginable. The assurance and peace that come from knowing him enable us to reach out to others, not looking, above all, to take, but to give sacrificially as he has given to us. He is the perfect friend who enables us to be true friends ourselves.

How sweet the name of Jesus sounds
In a believer's ear!
It soothes his sorrows, heals his wounds,
And drives away his fear.

It makes the wounded spirit whole,
And calms the troubled breast;
'Tis manna to the hungry soul,
And to the weary, rest.

Dear name, the rock on which I build,
My shield and hiding place,
My never failing treasury, filled
With boundless stores of grace!

By Thee my prayers acceptance gain,
Although with sin defiled;
Satan accuses me in vain,
And I am owned a child.

Jesus! my shepherd, husband, friend,
O prophet, priest and king,
My Lord, my life, my way, my end,
Accept the praise I bring.

Weak is the effort of my heart,
And cold my warmest thought;
But when I see Thee as Thou art,
I'll praise Thee as I ought.

Till then I would Thy love proclaim
With every fleeting breath,
And may the music of Thy name
Refresh my soul in death!

John Newton (1725–1807)

QUESTIONS FOR REFLECTION & DISCUSSION

- How does Christ forgive our greatest failings and meet our deepest longings?

- How can we avoid placing messianic expectations on our friends?

- In what ways has this book challenged us to be better friends? How does the gospel of Christ help us do that?

- How can we ensure that our friendships with other believers 'begin in Christ, continue in Christ' and are 'perfected in Christ'?

- What can we learn from the example of Christ as the perfect close, constant, candid and careful friend?

END NOTES

INTRODUCTION

1. Al Hsu, *The Single Issue*, (Leicester: IVP, 1998), pp. 137–138.

2. E. Ostrov and D. Offer, (1980) 'Loneliness and the Adolescent' in *The Anatomy of Loneliness* (ed. J. Hartog, J.R. Audy and Y.A. Cohen; New York: Simon & Schuster, 2000), pp. 170–185; quoted in Liam Golligher, *The Fellowship of the King* (Carlisle: Authentic Media, 2003), p. 3.

CHAPTER 1

1. Hugh Black, *Friendship* (London: Hodder & Stoughton, 1897), p. 25.

2. Aelred of Rievaulx, *Spiritual Friendship* I.33-49 (trans. Mary Eugenia Laker SSND; Kalamazoo, MI: Cicercian Publications, 1977).

3. James Wagenvoord, *Men: A Book for Women* (New York: Avon Books, 1978), p. 165.

CHAPTER 2

1. M.E. MacDonald, *The Need to Believe* (London: Fontana, 1959), p. 82; quoted in Liam Golligher, *The Fellowship of the King*, p. 12.

2. Nick Pollard, *Teenagers: Why Do They Do That?* (Southampton: Damaris Publishing, 2003), p. 47.

3. Joanne Harris, 'Why I'm ditching the internet', (*Daily Mail*, April 2010).

4. Tim and Kathy Keller, *The Meaning of Marriage* (London: Hodder & Stoughton, 2011), pp.120, 125–126.

5. Andrew Sullivan, *Love Undetectable* (New York, NY: Vintage Books, 1999), p. 198.

6. William Shakespeare, *Henry V*, Act 4 Scene 3.

7. Samuel Taylor Coleridge, 'The Rime of the Ancient Mariner'.

8. C.S. Lewis, *The Four Loves* (1960; San Diego, CA: Harcourt Brace, 1991), p. 80.

9. Hugh Black, *Friendship*, p. 3.

CHAPTER 3

1. John Frame, *The Doctrine of the Christian Life* (Philipsburg, New Jersey: P&R Publishing, 2008), p. 193.

2. Hugh Black, *Friendship*, p. 38.

3. Ibid., p. 158.

CHAPTER 4

1. Paul Tripp, *Broken-Down House* (Wapwallopen, PA: Shepherd Press, 2009), p. 152.

2. Jonathan Fletcher, *Dear Friends: Selected writings of Jonathan Fletcher* (UK: Lost Coin Books, 2012), p. 49.

3. Gordon MacDonald, *A Resilient Life*, (Nashville, TN: Thomas Nelson, 2006), p. 223.

CHAPTER 5

1. Hugh Black, *Friendship*, p. 169.
2. Lori Rentzel, *Emotional Dependency* (Nottingham: IVP, 1999).

CHAPTER 6

1. Robert Mack, *Happiness from the Inside Out* (Novato, CA: New World Library, 2009), p. 139.
2. Henri J.M. Nouwen, *The Inner Voice of Love* (London: Darton, Longman and Todd, 1997).
3. Henri J.M. Nouwen, *Reaching Out* (London: Fount, 1988), p. 9.
4. Francis A. Schaeffer, *True Spirituality* (Wheaton, IL: Tyndale House, 1979), p. 142.
5. Aelred of Rievaulx, *Spiritual Friendship* I.1.

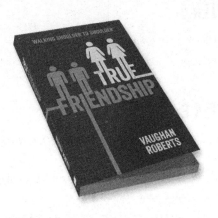

Publishing

a division of **10** of those.com

10Publishing is the publishing house of **10ofThose**. It is committed to producing quality Christian resources that are biblical and accessible.

www.10ofthose.com is our online retail arm selling thousands of quality books at discounted prices. We also service many church bookstalls and can help your church to set up a bookstall. Single and bulk purchases welcome.

For information contact: **sales@10ofthose.com** or check out our website: **www.10ofthose.com**